Is our planet warming up?

First published in Great Britain by Heinemann Library
an imprint of Heinemann Publishers (Oxford) Ltd
Halley Court, Jordan Hill, Oxford OX2 8EJ

OXFORD LONDON EDINBURGH MADRID
ATHENS BOLOGNA PARIS MELBOURNE
SYDNEY AUCKLAND SINGAPORE TOKYO
IBADAN NAIROBI HARARE GABORONE
PORTSMOUTH NH (USA)

98 97 96 95 94

10 9 8 7 6 5 4 3 2 1

British Library Cataloguing in Publication Data is available from the British Library on request.

ISBN 0 431 07640 5

Cover designed and pages typeset by Philip Parkhouse
Printed in China

Picture Credits
pp. 2-3, courtesy of NASA; pp. 4-5, © Bryan and Cherry Alexander; pp. 6-7, Pat Ortega, 1991;
pp. 8-9, © Ken Wardius/Third Coast; pp. 10-11, Mark Mille/DeWalt and Associates, 1991; pp. 12-13,
Michael Medynsky/Artisan, 1991; p. 12 (inset), Mark Mille/DeWalt and Assciates, 1991; pp. 14-15,
© Mark Edwards/Still Pictures; pp. 16-17, © Chico Paulo/Third Coast; pp. 18-19, © D. Houston/Bruce
Coleman Limited; pp. 20-21, © Mark Edwards/Still Pictures; pp. 22-23, © 1992 Greg Vaughn;
p. 24, © 1992 Greg Vaughn

Cover photograph © Science Photo Library/Jerry Schad
Back cover photograph © Sygma/D. Kirkland

Series editor: Elizabeth Kaplan
Series designer: Sabine Beaupré
Picture researcher: Diane Laska
Consulting editor: Matthew Groshek

Contents

Words that appear in the glossary are printed in **bold** the first time they occur in the text.

Exploring our environment

Look around you. You see deserts, forests, lakes and rivers. You see farms, factories, houses and cities. All these things make up our **environment**. Sometimes there are problems with the environment. For instance, the Earth's **climate** may be warming up more quickly than it ever has in the past. Rapid **global warming** could cause severe problems for all living things on our planet. Why is this warming trend occurring? Let's find out.

What was the Earth's climate like in the past?

In times past, the Earth's climate was very different from our climate today. For example millions of years ago, when dinosaurs roamed the Earth, our planet was warmer than it is today. In contrast, only a few thousand years ago, the climate was colder than today's climate. Huge sheets of ice, or **glaciers**, covered large parts of the Earth.

Such changes in climate are natural. They take place over thousands of years. Animals, plants and people can usually adjust to these slow changes.

What is happening to our climate now?

Today the Earth's climate seems to be warming up much more quickly than it ever has in the past. Since the late 1800s, the Earth's average temperature seems to have risen by almost 0.5° C. Some scientists predict that the average temperature may rise 1.5° C in the next 50 years.

Even a temperature rise of one degree in a few centuries is difficult for most plants and animals to adjust to. A jump of three degrees in half a century may kill off many living things. Many plants and animals may die out, or become **extinct**.

Holding in the heat

To understand why the Earth is warming up, you need to understand why it is warm in the first place. Our planet is surrounded by a thick layer of gases called the **atmosphere**. Sunlight passes through the atmosphere and strikes the Earth. The Sun's rays heat up the Earth's surface. The heat rises into the air. Some of the gases in the atmosphere, including **carbon dioxide** and **methane**, trap the heat and reflect it back to Earth. This keeps our planet warm.

What is the greenhouse effect?

The process by which the Earth's atmosphere holds in heat is known as the **greenhouse effect**. Like the glass that forms a greenhouse, the gases in the atmosphere let sunlight through, and like the panes of glass, the carbon dioxide and methane in the atmosphere hold in the heat.

Without these greenhouse gases, the Earth would be a cold, hostile place. The average temperature would drop below freezing. Life as we know it could not exist.

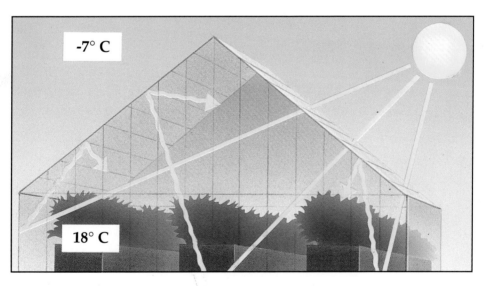

-7° C

18° C

Too much of a good thing

Greenhouse gases in small quantities are a good thing. But in recent years the amounts of carbon dioxide and methane released into our atmosphere have increased greatly. The Earth absorbs some of these gases naturally. However, the levels of greenhouse gases in the atmosphere are rising. Many people are afraid that the extra greenhouse gases will turn our planet into an uncomfortable hothouse, where living things will have to hide from the Sun's scorching heat.

Where do the greenhouse gases come from?

The extra carbon dioxide and methane in our atmosphere have one main source: us. When we burn **fossil fuels** – coal, oil and natural gas – we release these gases into the air.

Clearing and burning forests also increases the greenhouse gases in the atmosphere. Trees take in, or absorb, carbon dioxide from the air and combine it with water to make food for themselves. When large forests are cut down, there are fewer trees to absorb carbon dioxide, so the levels of this gas rise.

Are we heading for a global crisis?

Although the levels of greenhouse gases are rising, scientists disagree on how this will affect our climate. Some scientists think the Earth is not warming up rapidly and that we and other living things will be able to adjust.

Other scientists think that a rapid warming trend is upon us and we are heading for a global crisis. They think the world's farms will turn into deserts, and lakes and rivers will dry up. They predict melting glaciers will raise the levels of the oceans, flooding the great coastal cities of the world.

What can you do?

Power stations and cars release tonnes of greenhouse gases every day. So you can help stop global warming by using less electricity and by finding ways of getting about other than by car. Ride a bicycle or walk instead of going by car. Turn off lights when you leave a room. Ask your parents to turn down the heating in your house to **conserve** energy.

Another way to help halt global warming is to plant and care for trees. Because trees take in carbon dioxide, they are our natural allies in the fight against global warming.

Looking to the future

The problem of global warming cannot be solved in a day. It may take a long time to find clean sources of energy, such as wind energy, to replace fossil fuels. It may take a long time to replant the trees we are cutting down. But every little thing each person can do to conserve energy and to save our forests will help. Think about our planet. Think about ways you can help make the Earth a safe and comfortable place for the future.

22

Glossary

atmosphere: the gases that surround the Earth

carbon dioxide: a gas in the Earth's atmosphere which contains one atom of carbon and two atoms of oxygen; carbon dioxide traps heat close to the Earth

climate: the average or normal weather that a place has over a long period of time

conserve: to save; to conserve energy means to save energy by using less of it

environment: the natural and artificial things that make up our surroundings

extinct: no longer existing

fossil fuels: coal, oil and natural gas; these fuels formed from decaying plant and animal remains which were buried beneath the Earth's surface millions of years ago

glaciers: huge sheets of ice which once covered much of the Earth's surface; today glaciers are found in polar regions and near the tops of mountains

global warming: the rapid warming that the Earth may be undergoing due to increased levels of carbon dioxide, methane and other gases in the atmosphere

greenhouse effect: the process by which carbon dioxide, methane and other gases in the atmosphere trap heat near to the Earth, in the way that glass in a greenhouse traps heat inside the building

methane: a gas in the Earth's atmosphere made up of one carbon atom and four hydrogen atoms; methane helps trap heat near the Earth's surface

Index